The Moon

by Grace Hansen

abdopublishing.com

Published by Abdo Kids, a division of ABDO, P.O. Box 398166, Minneapolis, Minnesota 55439.

Printed in the United States of America, North Mankato, Minnesota.

052017

092017

 THIS BOOK CONTAINS
RECYCLED MATERIALS

Photo Credits: iStock, NASA, Science Source, Shutterstock

Production Contributors: Teddy Borth, Jennie Forsberg, Grace Hansen

Design Contributors: Dorothy Toth, Laura Mitchell

Publisher's Cataloging in Publication Data

Names: Hansen, Grace, author.

Title: The moon / by Grace Hansen.

Description: Minneapolis, Minnesota : Abdo Kids, 2018 | Series: Our galaxy |
    Includes bibliographical references and index.

Identifiers: LCCN 2016962408 | ISBN 9781532100536 (lib. bdg.) |
    ISBN 9781532101229 (ebook) | ISBN 9781532101779 (Read-to-me ebook)

Subjects: LCSH: Moon--Juvenile literature.

Classification: DDC 523.3--dc23

LC record available at http://lccn.loc.gov/2016962408

Table of Contents

How the Moon Was Made

The moon is around 4.53 billion years old. It is just a little bit younger than Earth.

Scientists are not certain how the moon came to be. Many believe that long ago a small planet hit Earth. Pieces of that planet and Earth broke off on impact.

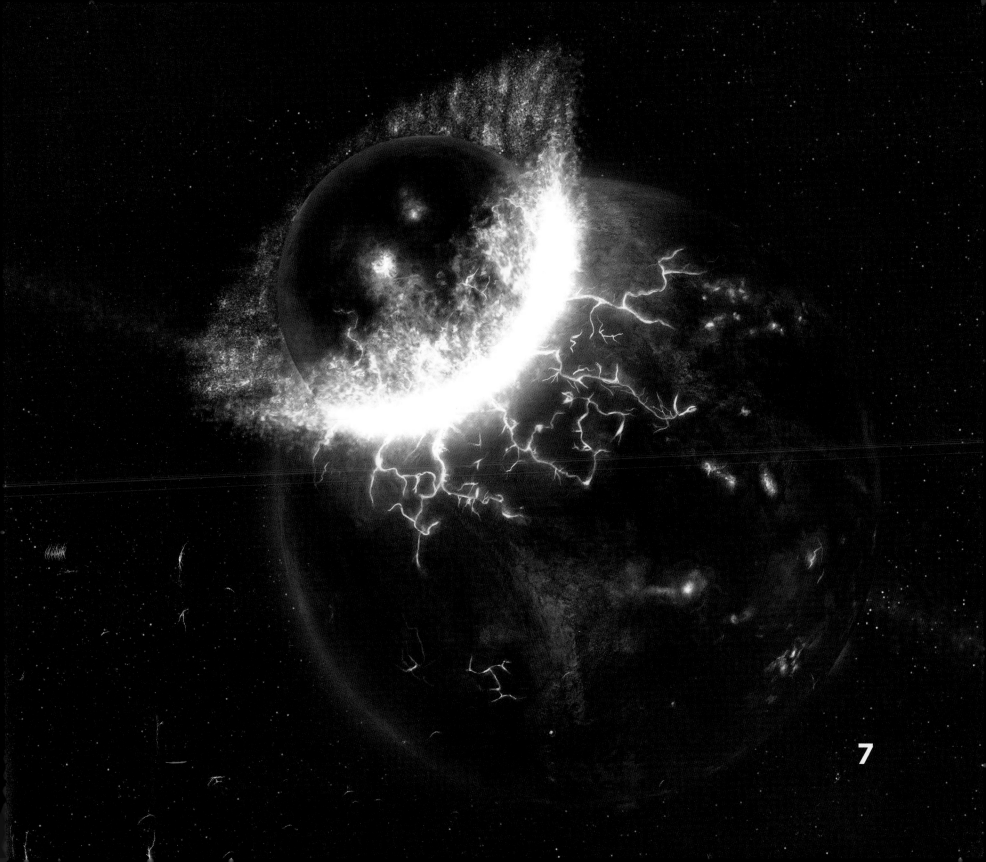

The pieces began **orbiting** Earth. Then **gravity** pulled the pieces together to form the moon.

The moon is the second
brightest body in our sky.
Unlike the sun, the moon does
not make its own light. It shines
by reflecting the sun's light.

Moon Changes

The moon looks different every day. This is because Earth spins while it **orbits** the sun. At the same time, the moon is orbiting Earth. All of this movement is constant.

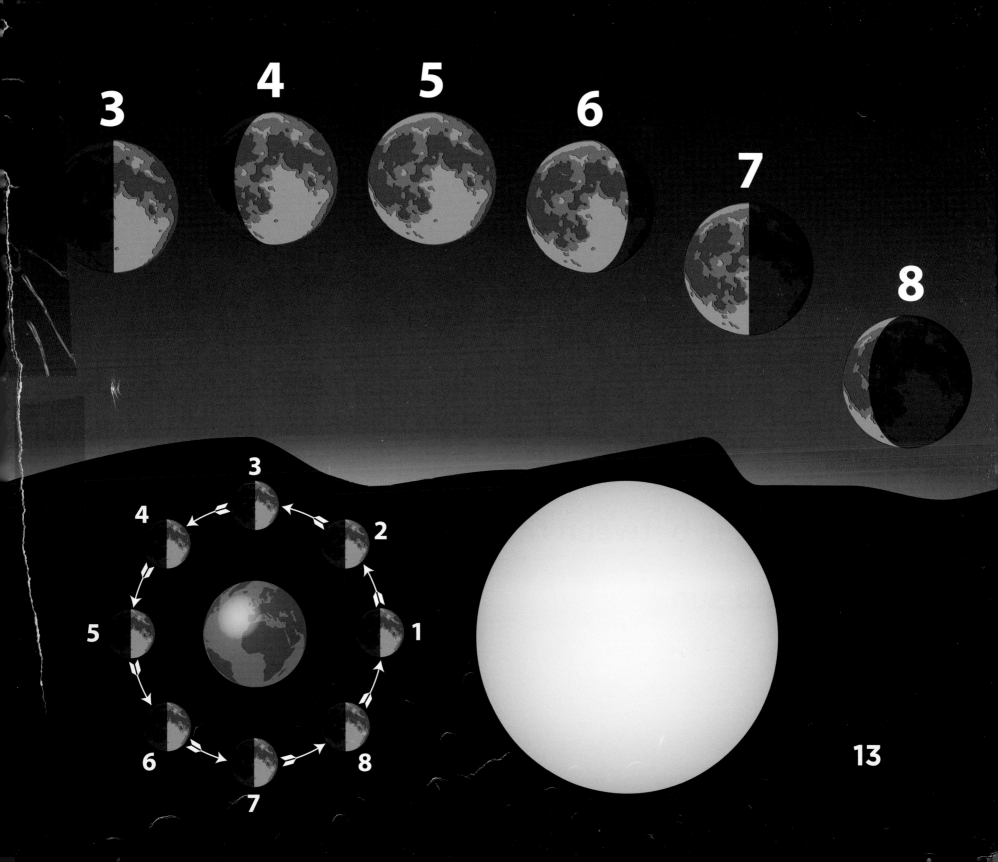

The moon takes about one month to fully **orbit** Earth. The new moon is the start of a new orbit. At this point, the moon is between the earth and sun.

sun

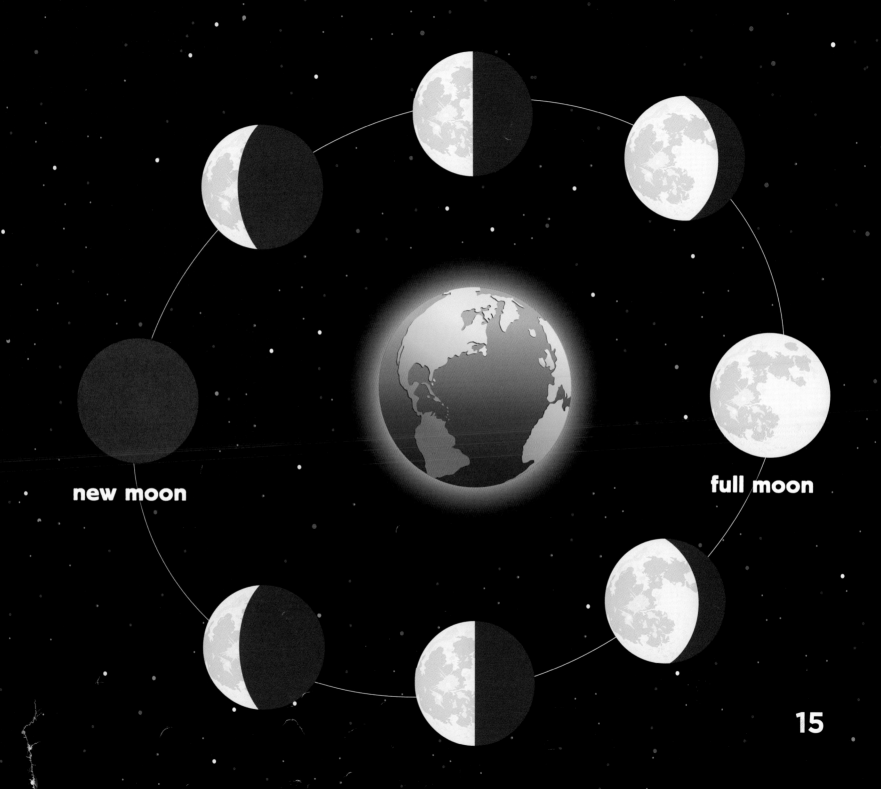

new moon

full moon

15

The moon is dark when it is between the earth and sun. This is because the sun's light is hitting the side of the moon we cannot see.

17

Around two weeks later, the moon is bright and full! Now the earth is positioned between the moon and the sun. The sun's light is shining on the side of the moon we can see.

Craters

The moon is big and beautiful. It is also a giant rock with lots of imperfections. **Comets** hit the moon long ago to make **craters**. The craters are easy to spot!

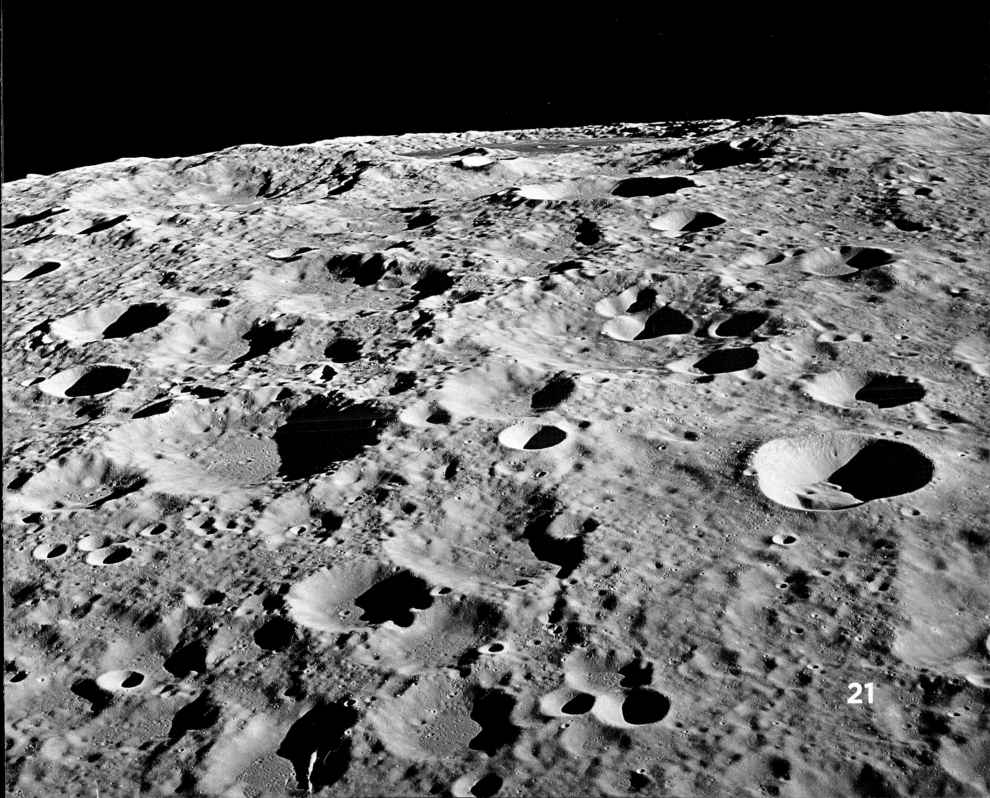

More Facts

- The moon is the only space body that **orbits** Earth.

- The moon orbits Earth every 27.3 days.

- On July 20, 1969, Neil Armstrong is the first human being to ever step foot on the moon.

Glossary

comet – a small space object made up of ice and dust.

crater – a large, bowl-shaped hole on the surface of a planet or the moon, typically caused by the impact of a celestial body.

gravity – the force by which all objects in the universe are attracted to each other.

impact – the action of one object coming forcibly into contact with another.

orbit – the curved path of a planet, moon, or other object around a larger celestial body.

Index

abdokids.com

Use this code to log on to abdokids.com and access crafts, games, videos and more!

Abdo Kids Code:
OTK0536

24

ML   DEC   2017